# Skinny Girls

# Skinny Girls

LESLEY-ANNE BOURNE

for Steve,
Even if you never
brought my coffee
or juice, you
are the best!
I miss you
already.
x Lesley

Banff '95

PENUMBRA PRESS

Published by Penumbra Press with financial assistance from the
Canada Council and the Ontario Arts Council.

ACKNOWLEDGEMENTS

Portions of this work have appeared in the following periodicals: *The
Abegweit Review, Event, The Malahat Review, The New Quarterly*, and
*Toronto Life*. Some poems first appeared in the following anthologies: *A
Discord of Flags, More Garden Varieties, More Garden Varieties Two*, and
*The New Poets of P.E.I.*

I am grateful to Don Coles, Laura Lush, Dale Zieroth, Sean Smith and
especially, Richard Lemm.

Thanks also to the Ontario Arts Council, The Prince Edward Island
Council of the Arts, and The Banff Centre.

Author photo: Richard Lemm

Canadian Cataloguing in Publication Data

Bourne, Lesley-Anne, 1964-
    Skinny girls : poems

(Penumbra Press Poetry Series; no. 31)
ISBN 0-921254-57-1

1. Anorexia nervosa – Poetry.    I. Title.    II. Series.

PS8553.0856S5 1993        C811'.54        C93-095133-6
PR9199.3.B68S5  1993

For Donna Bourne-Tyson

# CONTENTS

I. Creatures of Habit

# Creatures of Habit

INCHES FROM WHERE
   *(for Alistair)*

I'd gone to the hot springs
to swim that evening
but looking down
from the railing just above
the pool's slow bodies
there it was –
a child's blond hair
under water.

He looked about three
or four and nice,
a nice sort of boy
in a red bathing suit.

His little hands opened
and closed slower each time
through the few bubbles
(from his mouth)
floating the small space
to the surface

inches from where
his tanned parents dangled legs
on the pool's edge.

The hair still swirled
blond around his face.
I was glad I couldn't see.
One of the hands floated to the closest leg –
still laughing towards the man
she almost brushed the touch away.

CELEBRATION

The way the glass went off, broke, flew up,
and my mother's voice climbing the stairs

I didn't see it in her hand
or braiding the air between us
where she did my hair
every morning before I ran out

The glass, one of the small ones
I had my juice in,
tilted on the way down, spilling, and

fast and afraid I hit the steps and
looked down at the sharp pieces
neither of us
wanted to touch

things forgotten now
dribbled off slowly
but it was the way the glass burst

brighter than rage

We're insulating the cottage, my father
on the metal ladder, two rungs
from the top. Outside's raining loud
but I *do* hear
the first creak and
there *is* time –
even with small hands
I could steady it, & so
stop seeing his eyes see me
not moving or
not using my scared arms
to save us.
And the rain holds
my hands where they are
pushing so much thunder and
ladder and sharp roof pangs
ever after.

The news before bed
is a falling elevator.
At the last floor we
step out shaking
heads *not again.*
We are nothing
if not creatures
of habit. Take my mother.
Every cottage night
after my sister and I
climbed into bunks
having said goodnight to
my dad on the phone,
in the other room she
turned the radio dial
from static to static
till the British announcer
played "We'll meet again"
every show like the war
was still on. Vera Lynn
swayed with her while
the moths circled outside.
I never left the top bunk
but imagine her
near the wall
in a new dress, holding
a cherry coke
and tucking her hair
back as if some man would
ask her to dance.

On the eighth day of the heatwave
my mother packed it all
in new garbage bags

headed for town. A clean
start, she said. Yellow
machines spinning my pink

shorts and matching
tank-top, cigarette butts
tiling the floor.

How could she?
The lakeside loft where
she slept alone

that hot summer. Heat rising
till she couldn't stand
thoughts of him

in the city. Nothing cooled
leaves hanging off
endless nights. At Wash & Dry

I watched my sister
for signs – how long
would it take? She understood

magazines and hated
my mother's sandals,
out-of-style jumpsuit,

the way she wore her hair.
Most of all my sister
years older disapproved

of remote lakes when summer
desired a white-hot city
with no wife and kids.

Waiting for *you & your* car
is like that night
after ballet: class ended &
curtsies & thank you said
hours ago & a small me alone
outside in darkness. It began
snowing, slowly at first,
no real fear yet just
big stars that other times
I'd have trapped on my tongue.
Not tonight,
the freeway nearby, white lights
speeding closer, all my father
but then the red lights roar away.
Or a car slows
& I won't know what to do –
he's supposed to be here –
if he's not. His silhouette
lit by the dashboard,
the day's weight tugging
his face.
Aftershave in the warmth of
our station wagon, Oh
why isn't he here? Already
Mrs. Chamberlain has asked me twice
come back inside to wait but
that would make him
the one who's forgotten
what's to be done.
I'd rather stay here,
he'll drive up
any minute.

When we hear the swim-search siren
we run, undoing our clothes
as fast as we can
to the swimming area
where the siren keeps shouting

*

We may be at arts & crafts or
out canoeing – some of us
are sleeping in our cabins
when the alarm goes
that Sarah is missing –
still tagged into the pool,
the square marked off by docks
suddenly a larger square
now that she's missing

*

A few of us line the docks,
wait for instructions
and the siren to stop
Others search the island –
check paths and cabins
– maybe she's simply forgotten

the tag with her name
still on the swimming board
after everyone left the water
this afternoon

*

We break the water feet-first
the way we were taught
when they told us
– you'll likely never need this –

underwater, three strokes forward –
eyes always open
hands out
ready
for something
in the dark

hoping it won't be Sarah

*

one kick back
and again – fingers open
for the thing coming into them

the girl we hadn't really known
or even tried to –
the one we talked about
at night, flashlights
whispering enough
for her to notice

never wondering if she did

until now

*

from the deep end
the voice says in such a way

No

was partially missing.
No roof, I heard
at recess. Words
floated up like champagne

bubbles, burst in her head.
A spiral staircase
between rows of top teeth,
a never-ending climb. She

always tried as if
I could follow
the sounds to the room
no one else found. A room

at the very top of
her mouth where
the words crowded in, expectant,
waiting for the guest

who would understand.

In the pink tutu, she looks
like a ballerina, a young one
whose years end
in this photograph at seven.

Just after this moment so carefully framed
he would tell her
*I am a dancer too*
*Let me lift you* and his fingers
would go in.

She would not know the next moves,
had not been taught how to
hold her head, place her arms,
feet in the proper angles

and she would stay on his lap, let him
move her legs through positions
she'd never been warned about.

*Dancing made this happen.*
*I am bad for these pliés,*
*arabesques and the way*
*the pink satin and sequins now*
*press damp between my legs.*

The girl and her friend,
Claude, in the woods
behind the YMCA, skip lessons,

kiss. This is the deal
he's worked out
since he's older

by years. It hurts
but it's supposed to or
am I doing something I shouldn't?

His teeth, his wet mouth
all wrong. Try not to think
she hums, be over soon –

He has promised
his jack knife, the black one
he says, and next time

the red one.

Last night I dreamt you still bad,
your delinquent mouth as I
remembered, sucked in.
You were ten, the blond
on the block. I denied
playing with you by the creek
or in the bush – never
mentioned under the stairs
how you yanked and said
*feel me here*, your brown hands
giving a snake I wouldn't touch
and gifts – your cap gun or
baseball or something which
didn't matter. Your mouth
bullying mine. I'll give you,
I'll give
but there was nothing I wanted
except your brother to have followed
to find us
down in all that darkness,
that quiet, and I was
scared of that too.

Across the water
the boys' camp
is a dare they take.
After dark they dip

and stroke in canoes,
careful not to scrape
paddles against gunnels,
not to wet hair

or white T-shirts.
They've seen counsellors
do this, heard the guides'
cabins later. Derek from New York

knows she's coming –
his note with laundry pick-up
*I'd like to see you*

*tonight* wasn't asking.
Soon as they get to the docks
in the dark he'll lead her
through trees up the path

where he'll kiss as if summer
is real, as if a girl
isn't waiting on another island
back in his home state, as if

lightning across the lake
won't matter at all
once he takes her
as far as he wants to go.

Yesterday he drove his truck
through the church
to get her back.
That kind of devotion –
defying God

for love goes against mothers,
the Sunday school mornings,
everything before he met her.

She'd worn a polka dot dress
his favourite blue
and sandals.

Never kissed a girl
in gloves and a hat
before. She was in
the parking lot after service
let out. He played touch

football, the field behind
The Gospel Hall. Usually
couldn't wait for the religious
nuts to leave.
June smelled of grass
the sun warmed

all afternoon. At dusk
still warm. Her face flushed,
bare arms dangling
her jacket and little purse.
Lingering

she said something
he remembers the day

he floors it and crashes
through Ye Must Be Born
Again. Yesterday, there was

only the smell
on his hands and
the gear shift
and the wheel.

on a raft. Blue July
above as he stretched
a muscled arm over
her back.
Waves the boat tossed

loosened his grip and
the hand drifted down
where her bathing suit
stopped. The Mullens
inside making lunch.

He swam the cold lake
a lot the summer
they were sixteen. At night
the mosquitoes sung
when he snuck into

the guest cottage.
The dark smell of moth balls
and oiled skin.
He said he loved her
if he could

pull the sheet back.
A trout on the wall above.
Yard lights shined
the glass eyes. They were
still on the raft,

the small bed rolling
under his weight. She believed
water would wash over
everything or she could always
come up for air.

and I *had* been kissed. And
I was always hungry
but not for sex
which disappointed Teddy Filipovich
more than I can say.

There was that dinner he had
his mother's boyfriend (a chef)
set for my birthday, ready
to trap. Teddy,

as captain of the football team,
knew a lot of cheerleaders, knew
a few things when he asked for
pheasant, the wine, all that

chocolate sauce. What could I do
except eat and know
afterwards I couldn't say no –

after all, he'd waited
the whole term for this
knowing how I starved myself,
how good I could be.

What my bones
might be hiding – marrow so sweet
he'd drink. How could I refuse
a meal like that, another glass,
the sapphire slipped on

my slenderized finger while he whispered,
*sappheiros* making sure
I knew he spoke other languages
and the cheerleaders weren't lying.

As he opened his mother's bedroom door
he breathed *satiate, satisfy,* and
what he wanted to fill.
*Anorexia,* he whispered as if
this was my name, *such a shame*

*to leave these small.*

In grade eleven my best friends
Claire & Ruth stopped talking.
Their mothers' illnesses
drowned words. Cancer

of the breasts –
those things we'd hoped for
comparing after school
months earlier. Girls

contemplating a purchase
– new jeans, a sweater, oh
& two of those please,
large. Then later at college

a friend says the mothers
lived. At this I'm
back in Claire's yard,
the plums so blue

they were black.
Smooth skin, centers
where the stems rose.
The way they fit perfectly

in the hand.
The shrivelled
ones we called rotten –
thrown away.

are picked last
for volleyball, their serves
caught in the net.
Against gym walls they wait
for Marnie Neville's call
– Pam or Virginia,
sometimes Marion.

Their gym-suits
baggy, feet
size nine or ten.
In gymnastics they slouch
avoiding the uneven
parallels, fall
off the balance beam.

They're willows
in heavy rain, hydro
wires snapped by wind.

In the change-room
they seek private stalls.
The sharp-boned
shame they pull on
fits. For class photos

they're the back line
(with the boys
no girls want to sit beside
or dance with), legs
hidden by rows of
normal girls.

Or the Kerri's of the world
whose tight jeans get

called to the office
every week. Skinny girls
spend their lives standing

wanting what
they can't have. Rounder
breasts or even
breasts at all. Often
they're first to wear
bras, training
for a life of hope
one day they'll be liked

not for their mind.
Worst, they know it's
wrong... Older
and filling out, nothing
changes. Inside they're still

scrawny toothpicks. Why
does nobody believe?
So some skinny girls
do what they do best –
later you find them
gone too far.
In wards they're smiling
thinly as if
they knew you'd come back.

ten years her father's seen her die
almost. He still asks why
did she starve so long?
How? Under the hospital window
he thought she couldn't hear

*When can I trust*
*her again?* The nights
he'd sign her out for baseball
games in Lee Park, returning
at ten to the fourth floor

as if normal. His heart
breaking each time they passed
icecream stands. Or lunch hours
he walked from the office
to watch her not eat. In the past

ten years she's come back
a pound at a time.
He pretends not to count.
Playing catch in the yard
when she visits, they throw

fast balls and curves
without effort or hurting
each other that bad.

The first time they leave her alone
since the hospital, the station wagon
still backing out, she thinks about
telling them *It's all right*
*now. Promise.* Their fear and tiredness
pulling away from their youngest
who wouldn't eat or if she did
would vomit. Might as well
have been at our feet they used to say.
They've not yet understood that
those times she *was* hungry,
the food brought so hopefully
soured and spoiled part of her
ripening thinner and sharper
when they held her at night
afraid to dare sleep.
As the car hesitates forward
she wants to run out.
But that would frighten them too.
These careful days they all
watch for signs, make sure apples
have no razored lines.

Past midnight waiting for a train
reminds him how
he waited for a daughter.
In the anxious station
fathers pull out
what she'll look like,
their youngest; like you
they say. He loves
especially at a movie, her arm
slipped through the way
she used to reach his hand
crossing Main Street.
Rescuing his daughter now,
he takes the weight of luggage
from wherever she's been without him.
Those whole winters when
snowsuits tripped her!
Fathers were for that.
Ten minutes and she should be home.
Used to be he tried not to think
through all the channels
till car-lights came
and he could go to bed.

IF THERE'S TIME
*(for my father)*

The night war's declared
my husband and I are
at a movie
unaware. After,
in the parking lot
the snow is gigantic and still
we don't know. We
throw snowballs at blue cars
passing and wonder why
the drivers look like that.

And later our Lebanese grocer
Norman bundles oranges, says
My mother's there. Then
the news. Shortwave
from the back of the store
near the meat. So much
a pound, will that be
all? Would you like
to charge or pay? Jordan
he barely says as
we go. Outside
we don't know anymore;
the snow's all wrong,
too peaceful for this.
I can't look
at who held me
the whole movie and
turn away. A man
passes. Without looking

I know my father
though he's days away.
And the missiles
are the old ones

38

war unstopped
this time. He's been told
head for the underground room
with the others
picked to continue. A city
official, he's needed

they say, not his wife
his two small girls.
Back then I know nothing –
he comes home and steps
over toys and dolls
at five-fifteen as if
no one can change
his mind about where
he'll try to get to
if there's time.

I'm on the veranda
drinking gin. My
long white skirt
breezes in and out and
my arms are bare. Almost
evening, cocktails and croquet
if only I weren't alone. I am
my mother twenty-five years ago
waiting for my father
or after long enough, for
any man who will
pass by the front lawn
and unhinge the gate.
We are too young,
my mother and me, for this
much gin, all the whiteness
going to waste. And look
the sun promises
spectacular things,
even more after dark.
Perfect chances to warm
a cool summer night
while we lean against
loneliness and the ice-cubes
shimmer like diamonds
in rings.

## FOR BETTER OR WORSE
*(for P and T)*

Everyone I know got married
the hard way. City hall
on three days notice
while parents vacationed
in Hawaii or Hilton Head,
or in livingrooms
by a fireplace as
things went up in smoke.

Some went to dentists
right after as if
whatever needed filling
could be. Others
drove like mad
all night. Their wedding night
on the Quebec highway,
too tired when they checked in.

My sister climbed higher
than anyone, twenty feet
up a bell-tower.
In the lake breeze
we swayed, the wedding party
like patio lights.
When she said, I do,

parents on the deck
across the sand looked
happier. My mother
packing her trousseau
again, all ivory tulle,
my father washing the car, even
the whitewall tires.

A bay view porch
around my sister's house.
In sun we discuss to have
or not have
children, second

cars, next year
the Isle of Mann.
School uniforms used to
simplify. Now
whatever we wear

midday's too much.
On the white porch
we lounge in wicker, tall
green glasses dribbling water
the length of her arm.

Catalogue women
taped above cottage bunkbeds
long ago. At ten we
cared only about lakes
and tans. Now understand why

she started in on him
Friday nights driving away
from the city – cars,
kids, and just for once
a simple goddam vacation.

My sister yells
long distance as if
we've never grown up
or liked each other.

Grade ten again, Friday night
dance with Dan Hossler
in the dark gym
kissing me. On the bleachers

she watches until
it doesn't matter.
Never liked him
anyway, she says. When

I yell back now
what comes over
the wires is how
yesterday her van hit

a deer. The sound of
the weight, the colours.
She walked the highway
hoping the worst

hadn't happened. Somewhere
in the woods a deer
could be dying, she says,
she didn't mean it.

In the morning, the sunheat already
partway around the lake,
mother and the two of us
in the big wooden chairs
sport our nightgowns, pink
flannel shells in the eight o'clock breeze.
We glimmer as cars go by.
The smell of orange peel
churns in road dust & gravel.
We consider the calm water
while more cars pass and we
run out of orange.
The hot sun through our nightgowns
polishes the skin.

Another dream of you
ended badly. I couldn't change
your mind about someone
with longer hair and
bigger breasts, those
familiar skinny fears
coming true. All in your mind

I'd tell myself walking
right home after school
behind my sister, older girls
or Stephanie Reynolds who
disappeared into the woods
afternoons with a boy.

Aunts and my mother said
some boys don't care,
making it worse.

Sitting in my bedroom
wishing for a body that would
betray safe upbringings,
mothers, and a best friend
who agreed she'd never
like boys. I longed to

be the girl who
walked home late nights
thrilled by what he'd done.

The girl swooned, a
white tulle and lace
tulip in your arms. I

was the end. Your leaps
and grand gestures
the last time

I danced. Always
a swan dying, another
turn, one more perfect
arabesque balanced
long enough and then
the mad dive.

Some girls never learn.
Technique all emotion.
Sweat crystalizing pale
brows and small breasts.
The costume sewn shut
minutes before. I

used to look at you.
Anticipated in the wings
violins, the flute
a single note. And shadows

now of slender girls
come and go like snowdrops
caught on your tongue.

THE SKAGEN SOUTHERN BEACH
*(after a painting by Peder Severin Kroyer)*

First day of summer.
She's Anna, I'm Marie.
Bare feet.
1893 and evening
on the Skagen Southern Beach.

My husband's never seen
how we wander
this shore every day.
Not a promenade like
her husband painted
of five gowns, parasols.

We talk about men.
My friend's in love
but married
and so's he. Just then
a blind man walks by
where we've hid –

his white cane taps us
silent –
not deaf, what's he heard?
Our long skirts rustled
the Danish sand.

Anna won't look at me.
Marie, she says
squinting out to sea,
we'd better go
home. We hold hands
walking back – two
rendered women who lean
heads down as if
no one can hear.

Midsummer. The hydrangea.
Anna and I in the backyard
drink something tropical
while we discuss her fears.

They're men. The last one
hasn't written since
his wife found out.
Anna says she expected it

but swallows crushed
ice the tiny parasol garnishes.
How can I tell her it's okay
as the summer dress falls

from her bones? Too hot
too long, I finally say;
there's nothing else. She says
I love him, refuses

the past tense when I correct.
And who am I to advise
*I knew this would happen* or
*I'm sorry* or, worse,

*it'll get better?*
We drank all last summer
after a man left me –
said love didn't matter

like we believed it.
Wisteria and clematis,
we clung to
that rickety trellis.

Wrought iron chairs
a certain green
and a fringed umbrella tilted

over the bubbled glass.
Three straight days
without rain, warm afternoons
blazing nights.

Over coffee my neighbour
mentions again the emerald hedge
needs cutting, the rose

helped. Vines
through the trellis poke
their slender fans,

the middle of summer breezes
over us. Men from the past
lean everywhere. What was
I thinking? How could I have...

as if thoughts can finish.
Enough, she says
though I'm not sure of what.

I'm falling
down a well, & you're
a girl's best friend.
Know what to do? Run

back to my house
while singing & pick
lilacs along the path
the whole way. Race

for my closet &
slash the jungle of
pink prints & blue
dots to that particular

party dress. White collar
& lace cuffs with
pearl buttons, you know
the red velvet I wore

birthdays & recitals
you hissed through. The dress
chocolate milk poured on
by mistake. You said

sorry. Remember my party
gingerbread mansion
you destroyed
through its front door by

bullying? I used to love your
long hair & long-boned
arms & legs – the reed
of the Japanese

green & brown screen
at one end of the porch
we played monopoly in
all monsooning summer, you were

a bamboo wand of poison
I drank down
while you coaxed
every last drop.

last night she was swimming
at the YWCA with other
women. Bathing caps
dotted the pool –

looking down she
could have been any one
of the wives, mothers
arm after arm

or just floating. Chlorine
rose from the blue
cap. Her face coming up
submerged without sign

of anger or pleasure. What
would she say after
the year passed with no
letter? Why

was she swimming anyway?
The women kicking
as though shore was
close. Or open sea

finally after years trapped
in the harbour. I'd dreamt
all night to find her
swimming fifty lengths

without effort or breath
to say she missed
the other elements of earth,
fire and friendship.

I dreamt your daughter
had an aquarium
in her room. She and I
traced fish one night
through their neon swim,

her small fingers etching
the glass like skates
on ice. She thought
I was a friend.
You were out of town

your wife said
but I could wait. All night
the three of us watched
angel fish among ferns
and the fighting

fish. Your daughter explained
if you held a mirror up
the red-finned attacked
the reflection. Your wife
and I nodded

already familiar
with the need to separate
two sometimes.

TALL AND QUIET

Evenings we seek
a store for treats.
Wind picks up. A girl
lived here he says

(years ago I guess
keeping pace) I
kissed her there.
I look to see

which part of the body
though he means
geography. Then
way back to health class

films about women
or men but not both.
Where? I ask
hedges and white flowers

near stairs. Here
he touches my lips
as a tall and quiet
boy would.

In your old blue Volkswagen at night
how we lingered
wanting again the lights along
Rosedale in December –
those mansions offering
their twinkling red, blue and gold
security, happiness we thought or
at least love.
Snowfalls promise that, you said
believing at the time and
on a quiet globe-lamped dead end
you pulled over and
kissed me. Snow faster
around us and a car now
and then. I love you
I said to the man watching out
the brownstone's front window.
He stood there acknowledged
by tiny snowy lights glowing
on the white birch tree in the yard
a little sad and saying
*Come in. Love me.*

Last night we were in France
though you never knew –
you sleep so deeply.

Most of all you missed
the alleys,
miniature coloured lights

and men leaning
in restaurant doorways.
What could I do?

My French that bad – I
turned to you
for a quick phrase.

I kept hoping
you'd turn up
amid all the bells

on my scarf bought
in the metro, the bangles
a man slid over my wrist.

Tu es Américain? No
I thought, don't.
But I did. And you never

woke up. In bed
this morning you ask
from some far place,

would I lie about
something like Paris?

I'd race when I was little
to the edge,
braking my bike right before

the rocks below. I
didn't want to do it
– but the roar of

waves against rock,
water spraying
above. Once, I found

Nipissing's island
in rain. I stood
leaning on my bike

over my parents' last fight
as the downpour clouded
the view. I pushed

the tire forward,
little hands on the handlebars
certain the bike would or

the rocks or finally
the embankment
give out.

Sometimes when you enter
we become that day,
my bicycle, red and new

– if I pulled away
would you know
it's not what you've done?

The night before the worst
possibility, he goes out
while she watches
the game on TV.

A relief pitcher
jogs from the pen
just as she's afraid
the doctor tomorrow

will say something
bad. How her husband feels
is a mystery in a jazz club
downtown. She bets

he's scared   it's his
body, the lump inside
him. For once she doesn't know
the right thing, good

news not hers to say.
She'd give anything
– top of the eleventh
all tied, two on

and two out – if
the game would wind up
the way they hope.

It was Hawaii at night
when she ran into him.
A dream she thought

as he said let's go
back to my condo
where we can talk.

What about your wife?
she asked. She's gone
for hours he said I

told her you were coming.
You what? she said.
It's okay he said.

No it's not she
wanted to say but instead
they walked along

the water to a point.
The building was tall
& coral & on the top

floor the elevator opened
into the livingroom. I am
impressed she said

then he kissed her.
No not fair your wife
lives here I should

go. He led to the bed
& she knew then his wife
had come home & was

sitting in the corner
watching. Flowers around
her neck were white

like soft foam waves
far below the windows
the length of the wall.

Say the man's name
is Hank. The kind
in a diner or
the next greyhound seat
across the prairies.

Hank turns up this morning
as if I knew him –
dishes piled, the bed
unmade, I was about to
hang last night's laundry.

In wind and July sun
he helped with big things.
His hands shook,
smoothed and pinned.

Until now I was happy
just with clean clothes,
never really cared how
hands so large unwrinkle
everything out on the line.

*A friend of mine she cries at night*
*and she calls me on the phone.*
*Sees babies everywhere she goes*
*and she wants one of her own.*
– Bonnie Raitt, "Nick of Time"

At dusk the neighbours
play catch. I like how
on the spring grass
between them their baby sits

clapping. My friend would see
differently – she
wants a child but
with a man she can't

have. I see her with him
these days on the lawn
getting darker. The baby
chortles and waves

her blond head
as the baseball passes
from one to the other.
And so it goes until

someone drops the ball
or throws too high.
The baby waits. All quiet
a moment and then

it starts to cry
or does the woman?
Maybe it's the man
seeing love

but he won't
leave his wife
and grown children. What
can she do? She

rolls the ball slowly
to the baby. It bumps
a small foot
and stops.

He remembers she wore
a blue skirt, white blouse and
how her hair was
when they danced last
July. He's fond of
letters, writes regularly.
She recalls his wife
and a son.
Can she write back?
His truck on the highway
to the post office
out of town.
She sees the way
he hopes. And the son
who asks about *that lady*
*from the summer.*
At work she types.
Words darken as she remembers
*your breasts, there,*
*I've said it.*
She types
then whites out
how far things have gone.

Drive, she says –
it's enough. His heart
shifts while she
watches his hands
on the wheel turning
in the falling snow.
What will happen?
If she could touch
one of those fingers
she would but wonders
about buses and other
high vehicles seeing in.
His turn signal on
at the intersection
as if he's dreamed this
break in traffic.
Here's hope and
happiness for once.
The garden
he's driving them to.
He wanted to take her before
to the ravine near
the little bridge.
She also has thought
of the secluded trees.
They drive in silence,
a nice quiet as if
the road doesn't have to end.
Here they are –
go slow. Through trees,
the mansion with the gates and
windows where parties
shined or fireplaces
quietly warmed. They've stayed
minutes too long

and so continue.
No one around. She's heard
at times the garden's busy.
Must be summer she thinks
as snow begins again
to fall. She's wanted
the empty branches, winter's
sky and an afternoon
like this. She wishes
she could tell him. He's
wishing things too
at the bridge. Not frozen yet,
water wets the crystals
falling harder. They cannot speak.
Four boys in the distance
approach the car.
One carries a football; he
could be his son, same age.
Even looks a bit like him
she thinks while looking at
the face steering.
He's thinking of children
they'll never have
and how they'd look like her
face turned towards him
now. Drive, she
or he whispers
amid other impending words,
as through snow the trees
and the river run.

# The Waltz

Camille Claudel at nineteen became Rodin's pupil. Later she became his model, mistress, muse and collaborator. For almost ten years she produced masterpieces of her own while influencing many of Rodin's sculptures. Controversial theories hold that some of Rodin's works were conceived and crafted by Camille but were signed by him.

After Rodin refused to marry her, Camille ended their relationship. She tried to continue with her art but suffered an emotional breakdown. Her family committed her to an insane asylum where she stayed until she died thirty years later.

Reine-Marie Paris, the granddaughter of Paul Claudel, Camille's brother, is the author of *Camille, the Life of Camille Claudel, Rodin's Muse and Mistress*, which contains photographs of the artist's work, letters and documents.

Some of the poems in "The Waltz" contain quotations from Paris' book. Many of the titles of poems in this section are titles of sculptures.

THE BATHERS

*You can't imagine*
*how pretty it is*
There is a park
close by and the river,
Madame Courçelles assures me,
may be bathed in
without the slightest danger
at the narrowest part
where her daughter
and the pretty maid
undress

THE LITTLE SIREN

And Rose, does she know
of your promise
to buy me
*a little bathing costume*
*– dark blue with white*
*piping, two pieces,*
*blouse and pants*
(you know the size
don't you)
*at the Louvre or*
*Bon Marché*
*or at Tours*

## WOMAN AT HER DRESSING TABLE

As a child on lime-treed afternoons
I dreamt I'd find
I was pretty     Beauty's
out of reach, but why not
like those tea roses –
crimson, soft-pink?


## BUST OF A WOMAN WITH CLOSED EYES

These days Rose must be trusting
the nights like those early ones
of ours

Water lapping with
only a little sound,
the enclosed place –
We could compare waves, size,
number of starfalls

PSALM (YOUNG GIRL WITH A HOOD)


God, listen,
things might have been
better      Henri might have
lived      Everyone can use
an older brother
to practise on



DEATH OF A GIRL WITH DOVES


My brother would understand
how that stranger,
the hot August morning
when the peach tree did not move,
opened the gate      Look,
I've tried with oil on canvas
how she just lies there,
a bare arm stretched out
while six white doves
cover her

*She picks light like a bouquet. Rodin presents it in a compact block.*

From where we are by the water
there is night, trees,
he holds my hand
He more boldly
samples the smoothed surfaces
than I do     A little piece of
wood drifts to make a petal,
warm, rounded, the small shape
as blameless as
what he cups, oh,
many nights still

CLOTHO (THE FATE)

The gods hid
rivers in my blood     You know
men wanted to bathe inside me,
swallow the warm liquid
clear     I think I floated them
away from weeds and lilies
they didn't know how to trust

## THE GOSSIPERS (DETAIL OF MARBLE-AND-BRONZE VERSION)

Even my own mother
calls me his concubine
But she's wrong
Every day in broad sunlight
(not even waiting till darkness
hides us all)
the public *has* me
– I am every man's,
anytime, always
The brocade ropes
stop nothing


## MAN WITH HIS ARMS CROSSED

Admire the murderer
for what he's done
Watch how he looks at me;
how unashamed he focuses
those small places     The ones
you take a step towards

MATURITY

Ripe, that's what he'd moan
when he entered
the clouds and burst them
The swollen fruit      Here
I am again where
he wanted me – on my knees
If you'll kindly form
a group to the left
I'll take you through
the way a lover
should, slowly      An old man
led away by *an old hag*
while a young girl tries
holding him back      On her knees,
those childhood scars – pink
maps marking the way


THE WALTZ

Her head tilted to
his shoulder and his lips
near      Soon he'll step back
His left foot
shows that      La valse
ladies and gentlemen,
finished      I am
the gift he gives
Fritz Thalow      Do you think
he'll dance me too?

I'm in room six
*They've begun installing*
*the central heating*
*Workmen all over*
*the house     Scaffolding all*
*over the courtyard     Once*
with my brother Paul
running through the garden's
blossoms, by accident
he touched my breast
This startled
the lilac air
and we ran     He cried
further on     *You see how*
*many difficulties there are*
*in this asylum, and who knows*
*if it won't get worse*
*in a little while*

FIRST STEPS

I walked later than some
of my family Did I guess
how far away
I'd be happy?
No thoughts of Mother's
disapproval or Louise's
scorn entered the boulevard
with the untamable
garden       He
cut off my feet
for his work, my hands
I settled at La Folie Neubourg
amid the half-ruins, haunting
the vines, cracking stone


LOUIS-PROSPER CLAUDEL

Paul will not answer
my letters       Only my father
never forgot
the little girl by the gate,
taking her hand,
the raspberries in her fist

SEXUALITY


I'm displayed to the
white-coated patrons
passing by     After
*Balzac,* I wrote to him
*I also like the idea of*
*the empty sleeves*     Doctor,
my father died
thirty years ago     Do you see
where my hand is
meaning?



BUSTE DE RODIN


I stopped at love     A silly place
to stop,
I know now

## THE ALSATIAN WOMAN

Terracotta with
a silver patina –
she's not me
I'm not mad
although there are hallways
where I'm wishing
I was
Figures like this one, bulging,
chunked, line up in them,
their bodies lean over me

DREAM BY THE FIRE

"I weep for the disappearance of
the dream of this dream"     Debussy
played for me
in the dark     I sat
at his feet while they pedalled
happily     Back then,
before he met his young
prostitute, I was his
demoiselle élue
He chose me

STUDY OF A MAN'S HEAD

I kept making them
out of clay     Bismarck,
Napoléon I,
David, Goliath –
when I was about fifteen
Later I tried Auguste R.'s
profiles     Of all these
men, some were successful

others not

## YOUNG ROMAN

My brother Paul at sixteen
What I've always needed
but couldn't have     *Le Frère*
*et la soeur*
lasted longer
When he visits here
I'll ask him, Do you
remember those huge black rocks,
the horizon always dark?


## ETERNAL IDOL (L'ÉTERNELLE IDOLE)

"I showed her where
she could find gold,
but the gold she finds
is truly hers"
Gold? Look around
There's only this tree
close to my room's
crippled window

## WOMAN KNEELING BEFORE A HEARTH

Locked up at my age
where's there to go
except childhood
When Jessie and I
shared the studio
in Paris, she was pretty

Oh, one thing more
Don't make too much of it, but
she didn't abandon me


## SHE WHO WAS THE HELMET MAKER'S BEAUTIFUL WIFE

How she suffered

Everyone's heard how
on his deathbed he asked
for his wife

But they wouldn't let me in

## IF THINGS HAD BEEN DIFFERENT, CAMILLE WRITES
## TO RODIN

My favourite creature
the elephant never
forgot. A girl,

I was thinking you
would be like that.
Lilacs by our house

rained purple every spring
right about now. A boy
kissed there once,

so French lilac bushes
or certain perfumes
make me stop. The way

you do. No,
you don't. Haven't
heard from your city

since the snow. Things
change a lot underneath
all that time. Crocuses

lead up to the house where
I live with a man.
As much as I can I don't

think about the weather
or parts of the body
I miss more than seasons.

# Finnish Scenes

The Art Museum of the Ateneum is in Helsinki, Finland. It celebrated its one-hundredth anniversary in 1987. Some of the poems in the series are based on paintings found there, and on the history of Finnish Art.

Turku is the former capital of Finland. Both Helsinki and Turku had active drawing schools in the eighteen hundreds.

Fredrik Cygnaeus, a literary historian and member of the Finnish Art Society which was founded in 1846, worked to create a Finnish Art Academy.

Nothing special; he travelled me
from the Art Academy
in Stockholm via

Paris and Italy
back to Stockholm
and Turku. He was

*the kind of man*
*Turku had longed for.*

you wanted me
in a room above
the restaurant open
every day of the year.

Every day, think of it;
how busy I was with you,
how willing! Garlic crept
up the stairs at night.

Sometimes you'd bring
flowers, sometimes not.
A bottle of wine always.
I couldn't drink enough

and longed for days
when fruit trees would curtain
the street you lived on
– those petals piling

like snow you waded through
each step as the door
drew back inside where
I slept.

I think about you at night
when I sleep. Always you're

near the railing, one arm
resting, the other around

a woman I know. You never
see every night the ship

pulling away from the harbour –
all the lights ripple then

disappear.

Saturdays are museum days.
The Ateneum opens at ten. I manage
the rainy steps too early
every week. The guard smiles
unlocking the big door.

In the shop I
check new things, see
if you've been there. Your hand
close. Some days one or two women
move slowly, look
at everything sadly as if
they know you too.

Coffee is good, also
the small cakes. Tables
for two, the size
I'd like if you did
walk in at ten
with no other
place to be till four.


ATENEUM GUIDE


basing itself on central women (I
mean of course works of art) and
lovers (I mean artists) in the
collection, the guide offers a
cross-section and a view to the
development of unhappiness
(no, I mean Finnish art)

"Winter is not for the painter an abomination...
his sensation of this translucent whiteness is
as sweet as the rustle of one's mistress's silk
skirt as she approaches."
– Fredrik Cygnaeus


These snowy tracts
know nothing about why
I walk late afternoons
when the light's changing.

Mornings I hate
everything, noon
not much better. After four

*you* wander back
into thoughts as a child
who's tobogganned
all day in the snowfall

will, his knitted hat
and blue mitts wet
then frozen
in the shape of hands.

## PORTRAIT OF THE ARTIST'S SON

Look at him
staring from the balcony,

pink flowers beside
his head. You've painted

too well. He will
grow up, have his heart

cut once and then the world
will be less again.

## FRUIT TREES

The white blossoms opened
like freesias you gave
years ago. In the water
and vase they leaned
back as if they'd waited

a long time for you.
The slender tree trunks
carved the grass
and branches hit ground
when they saw you with her

walking away from the tent.
The red and white canvas
stripes burned a grey sky.

and shadows from where I watch
you swim. Every day in the pool
your favourite's the front crawl,
sometimes side-stroke and then you
lie on your back. I move more into shade as you splash past –
often I'm holding your blue towel
against my face when you open your
eyes underwater. You can't see what
I'm saying into the cotton and when
you dry yourself later, the words
will bead on your skin.


## STORM ON LAKE NÄSIJÄRVI


Where were you
that summer the cottage
burned? Lightning,
July '72. The whole lake
lit up – cars
from the other side
drove over, volunteers
stayed till five. Smoke
rose all day – the smell
in wet leaves, blackened
ground. I walked up
and down the road-side
weeds growing over while you
were a storm gathering.

That close to Russia,
still, I couldn't
board the train
alone. Not to mention
ships all night rolling
closer to St. Petersburg.
At the station
I priced tickets, times,
bought postcards to send you
never sent. Small glass
birds sold beside chocolate,
men planning to drink
their way to the Winter Palace.
Always thought I'd meet you
there one morning
in light snow, no wind
to speak of.
        Love
renders cities, whole
continents unreachable
in good weather, let alone
peace time.

Speaking from experience
all it takes is a new moon
or his face

to make her risk
the bright painted current –
the Prussian-blue water
over her head as

migratory, she follows
the field-rush of his eyes.

Crescent-shaped seeds
& black fruit tangle &
pull her down.

June in Mukala was
mostly rain, some sun
and small boats
in the harbour. No one
looked like you
till later, midsummer
when the sun never
quit. That time
the bonfires lit
every island and I
was a cruise ship
not far off. Smoke
flamed into the night
sky that wouldn't go
dark as kayaks paddled
closer. Children
on the boat ate sausages
and laughed while German
men drank beer and stood
against railings as you.
But of course you
never were in Finland or
sincere. For you
the sun always sets.

To Madagascar

She watches through overcast
his plane taxis off. Silver

she'll remember later as
the last she saw of him. He

sits near the front of the jet,
one small window his face –

tired and closes his eyes
as the 747 slowly heaves

his thoughts in the direction of
home. Turned away,

the plane has forgotten the girl
leaning against the terminal glass

while the drizzle picks up.
A roar drowns out

what they did and what she'd say
if he was beside her;

it kills I love you
said just now

next to take-off.
The wheels start

the final stretch before
the air, where, in his mind she is

a departure
from his other life.

THE WAY I LEARNED OF YOUR LEAVING

the water is down this year
you said
waves only lift so far


IN THE APPLE ORCHARD AFTER YOU'VE GONE

What can I tell you
that's not been said
by better women.
How many? Don't forget
the ones in stairways

as you kissed your way
to the car, or
all the brunettes
as elevators closed
going down. For long enough

I believed perfect apples
didn't fall for anyone else.
You had me there
in the orchard
that time and another

as if you could reach
and pull one
over on me as often as
you liked under branches
anyone would have seen through.

You're gone two days
and still no letter.
How humid it is;
nothing makes sense.
Watered the plants twice
today, couldn't stop
believing them thirsty.
We lean together
into shade, any available
coolness under trees
or a white café umbrella.
I'd even take refuge under
a strange man's shirt
taken off in the heat
if offered and held
like a canopy, high enough.

Her study window faces
five trees. No leaves
yet, the bareness reminds her
of times he flew
back to his life. Mornings
the coffee was weak
and the paper late.
Front page news depressed
anyway, backruptcy
and loss. She searched
the stock market for
word of where he was
now. Over
land or water, if he
crashed this minute
would he know how to
swim? In the kitchen
she'd practice diving
the way it's taught –
with her head up
above water, eyes
on his body
every second

We'd split after less than the year.
Out here we look for signs,
see how bad the dryness is
and whether it will be fixed.
You can't imagine how yellow the grass it,
how flimsy the earth's become.
When it's windiest
dust runs my hair back
the way you would on our bed
with the rain against the window
moving down and down
and down. What do you do where you are
– out here there's no rain
though they tell me daily
leaning closer, it is coming.
We check for clouds, the wrong side of
leaves, sometimes even a newspaper –
but forecasts are never right,
are they? You and I said
they'd be wrong
(their own lives out in front like
 a branch
 witching for a well)

WHAT I LIKED MOST:


sleeping the afternoons when
you read in the next room.
Pages turning or not
I was willing back then.

The sun angled and left.
You got up once, no, twice,
made tea, jotted notes
about the novel: *nice.*

A love story, I learned
later. Turns out the notes
were letters to
a woman before

who'd fallen asleep listening
in the just-steamed air
to papers, your hands and
the sun going down.

In the pine forests
of Provence I hunt
you even if the forest
comes from books. Fire
in a friend's livingroom,
a fine Côtes du Rhône while
outside snow's begun.
*Look*, I say pointing
through trees as if
she can see your face
between branches. Then
again, she's accustomed to
travel and wine
and hearts that refuse
scrub oak from
the Luberon or
beech
from the Ventoux foothills.
I've stopped on the Bonnieux road;
it's you I cannot
pass. *The mistral*
she warns, *gets you*
*every time.* What does she
know of wind or stone?
*C'est normal* she says
pouring reason into long-
stemmed glasses. Trees.
Lavender plants,
asparagus, the boulangerie
at Lumières where I
fell so hard for
a good bordeaux.

Let's say we are
Lili and Vladimir
trying to meet
in Berlin. Much depends on
the post each morning.

Lately my dreams don't work
out. And the rain's
not come. Also the postman
altered his route. I'm last
waiting on the stairs.

*Are you hiding
the beauties composed for me?*
Listen, as he leaves my lawn
the postman kicks tiger lilies
like he knows

something. As if he's read
Mayakovsky and understands
Russian well enough to know
how his letters end.

The man walks away
under the chestnut tree
as the white petals fall.

There's a blue air-mail
envelope in his hand
to get her back, hoping
he'll catch the last
run at four o'clock,
it won't be too late.

What she's doing right now
he can only guess as
more floral remnants
rain down the way
her most recent letter
had. *I don't love you
anymore. I want to end
this.*

If only he can reach
her before the last petal,
if only she could see
the flowers grown-up,
big white candles
(she'd called them)
on the tree in the yard.

Evenings when they sat close
in the slow wooden swing
the small flames burned safely
like on a Christmas tree
seen long ago in Finland
he'd always hoped to bring back.

While you've been away
I've gone mad.
Ripped out the flowers
blooming red and purple
you like. Dirt
scattered over the green
green lawn you left
without word.
You flew in the morning.
That night I watered
all the plants
with the yellow hose
bought together before
your big plans. If I'd known
I'd have picked another
colour – you'd hated
yellow as a girl. I didn't
know. His name
is familiar and not
surprising, I even like him
though not as much as you
do. Each night at dusk I
water what's left.
Petals wave back
almost like you're upstairs
moving towards bed.

*"The three pear trees looked different. The
articulation of every branch had become
apparent, I could see how each leaf moved."*
– John Berger

Your letter this afternoon opened
the storm, the all-morning-waited-for
small signs of rain and then
the drizzling
rest of the day. Undoing
your letter by the window,
not wanting any words to fall out,
your voice pelting down,
darkening sidewalks, lawns,
whole sentences across windows.
I watched all this.
Now your words are all over
the fast-flooded landscape.
When the creeks' panicked levels lower
I will write to you slowly, explain
the roads we may still have.

I have decided to tell you
what sound loss makes.
These last days
before your counted-on departure, violins
move through the rooms slowly
like fan-tailed tropical fish,
colours billowing
as easily as the near-summer wind.
The summer you will miss.
Men on the street
look like you, their eyes
full of leaving, whole scenes
of lovers going away,
opera closings,
awaited denouements.
Their hands are just as bad –
open as if emptied right then
of a breast or other parts,
the palm's unfolding is
the catastrophe. We expected
the way it was discordant
near the end, but just before
that moment
we can never take back
did you hear
the branches arch
toward the snow?

But how can you answer me now

Amid dwarf peonies
from Siberia, marigolds
and Virginia bird cherries
near the small lake
the hotel gives way to,
it's the eighteenth
or nineteenth century.
I'm the woman in the bath.
Below, you are just now
completing a long trip.
It took years, others
got lost, not everyone makes it
here – I don't need to remind you.

Forgive me. It's just that
the window's open
anticipating someone tall.
You cross the esplanade
and enter the lobby's dark
wood and brass, all the
ferns flourishing
and the elegant fan
whirling. Your thoughts
having made it
past the French chairs'
palest pink silk
and Sir John Soane's
drawings as fast as
you could run.

## BLACKBERRY PICKING

August blackberries grab
when we walk
the last weekend. Almost over,
summer sulks on
coarse vines as
tree toads buzz air.


## VINES

Like the last time
(even the rain the same
and the dark as dark)
you turned to me.
Could've been that summer
when thunder started
far enough away. I thought
the usual – the storm
will miss us. Sometimes
whole fields lie drenched.
Others wait thirsty.
In the vineyard
the grapevines cling
to one particular night
when the rain came
warm and fast then
left them
wanting more.

Matisse could render
how light picks up red

in a room. Could be
these are flowers

he had in mind, the tender
afternoon. Would he

think about long stems leaning
the girl against him? The sun? Or

leaving. All of it
black and fire. She says

Don't paint anything. Instead
you could do something

like stay.

Let's say this is metaphor.

On one side of the highway
hundreds of snow geese

paint the small grass hills.
The other side just as crammed

with a blizzard.
I am the car stopped in the middle

of what you've left. Faraway
this evening, do you sense

how white it was
those nightfalls? Remember?

You leaving rendered everything
bare.

Let's say I didn't love you,
better yet, say snow geese

come back.

Can hardly think of you.
Ice this morning
feather-edges windows
the way I shaded
maps in grade eight
geography. Mr. Tilson
the man I loved.

Edges were lines of blue
water, bodies of it
everywhere. So much water between
you and me. Back then
coloured pencils – greens, browns
and blues – seemed enough.
Lines on a map,

which way to go
was easy. Goodbye
never is, is it?
Not like colouring or
sailing to Madagascar.
You're as far
now. The ice-

shaped continent shines
as a diamond
when sun hits.
Meanwhile, in places, small
cold mountains build up
dangerous crevasses
to fall into anytime.

*I love you.* He's sent
a photo of summer,
his last letter
as his wife slept.

Her husband's called to her,
does she want tea? What
does she want? Summer
rained more this year
than she remembered,
reminded her how lush

grass is, just how deep
the green of trees
can be. How wet
outside gets. Dangerous
having summer this close
she thinks and touches
the glossy 4 × 6 forest.

Even then he captured
more than rain
on her blouse, hair across
her face staring out at
why he took the picture.

Oh I am flying
from you fast! Bolted
steel withstands more –
celestial mountains
and a river
I cried over you.
No. Just some water
and grass fields
unfolding quilts
over our afternoons. No,
never again. Snow-
falls descend peaks
the plane shadows. You were
the best thing to happen.
We were a land faraway.
Below, trucks and
children don't know
anyone grieving on this
morning flight. Just like
I don't know you look up now
from your office desk
as I blaze
headlong into the past.

Here on the American west coast
the pianist looks familiar.
And he's playing
*You belong to me.* I
try the cajun shrimp, another
champagne and escape outside.
This is not easy
in heels. The rain's stopped
on the heavy flowers,
their lavender scent.
Now he's blue, bluer
as water starts again.
O where are other guests? Anyone
who will guide from this patio
and all the strawberries
silver-trayed and sliced,
small hearts open.

Surrounded by oceans I
think mountains & you

are the man at the top
most nights. The light

through trees means you
read or paint or

someone's there.
Thoughts avalanche. I

flick them off, prefer
the dark especially

when you're not on a map
I can unfold & hold.

But sometimes you're here
at the edge of the bed

after nightmares
I had as a girl –

your cool hand
on my forehead.

Other times you know
you drive me to them.

The Mexican men's soccer team
sings outside
three floors down.

In the hotel we're neighbours
touring but
their music's sad

for you who are elsewhere.
Heavy red flowers each time
I want you

start another song
before the next match.
Strange, our building's

heat's switched on
though it's seventy-six
in shade – maybe not

to warm the track-suited
serenaders at all, is it
to rain white

mechanical hum over
heartfelt songs I hear
lamenting the loss

of you?

In Ontario a train's
eclipsing a lake right now.
Aqua waves foam
the train's left side
as on a ship crossing
between England & France
Christmas Eve '84.
Six stormy hours. Enough
already, I told the god
in my head. The train
curves from the last car –
see what's come before?
Every passenger,
the engine. You've been
the prophet too long. On trains
or water. Protector
of the traveller
night & day, crossing
the channel I prayed
your name & memory.
God save me from
you & the waves.

## AT THE WINDOW

Thinking about a child I
toss & turn nightly.
But then morning quiets
the dark cries. Tired

my husband & I jostle
for coffee & news of
the latest war. Across
our yard frost paints

a black roof. I look at
houses for signs of
infants – light such as
a child's lamp

spills. Do mobiles
and toys shadow
all the houses? I
transcend as CBC

says *Now, summing up...*
meaning seven a.m.
not life. Mine
& his & what?

The snow will come
any day. By then
I should know.
Every woman must stand

one clerestory morning
at the window
sure that small, hot lips
breathe her neck.